Easy Drama
Lessons

Easy Drama Lessons

Written by a teacher, for teachers

Catherine Rix

Table of Contents

Introduction

This book is not intended to be a philosophical thought-provoking piece debating the value of drama and its place within the curriculum, the purpose is simply to provide teachers with ideas and some resources.

If you are already a confident practitioner, familiar with teaching drama and you are looking for some inspiration then skip this introduction and go directly to the practical tasks. However, if you are less experienced, or are yet to be convinced of the value of using drama as a vehicle for learning, I suggest you spend a few minutes reading the following, before plunging into the tasks.

Drama as a tool for learning - why?

Young children learn and make sense of the world around them through play and imaginative exploration. Venture into any nursery or early years classroom and you will find representations of a shop, a café, a kitchen… These structured learning areas provide children with the opportunity to practice and develop language skills, social conventions, critical thinking… The exchange of empty cereal boxes and plastic fruit allows numeracy to be used in a 'real' setting, while the young customers in the mock up restaurant and coffee shop use literacy skills to consider menus and waiting staff note down make-believe orders on pads of scrap paper.

Let's clear up a few misconceptions.

Drama is not theatre.
Drama is not about being an actor, it is about imagining, empathising and questioning.
Drama does not require a box of props.
Drama lessons do not need to last for an hour or more.
Drama lessons do not require large empty spaces.

On the plus side…

Drama provides students with the opportunity to think about, feel and experience situations which allows the expansion of their analytical skills, emotional intelligence and vocabulary.

Writing within the context of a drama lesson provides purpose and a real audience. The nature of group tasks removes the pressure of 'getting it down on paper' but ideas can still be contributed and thus provide all students with a positive experience and sense of fulfilment.

Drama is cross-curricular. Drama lessons are not and should not be restricted to the English Department, links with the Humanities are probably obvious but even the Maths Department can become involved!

Reluctant readers don't realise they are reading, and reluctant writers don't realise they are writing.

I could wax lyrical for hours and pages about the virtue of using Drama as a tool for learning, but if I haven't lost you as a reader, I suspect you are itching to get at the good bits, so I will leave you with one last point, to persuade anyone still wavering: there's a lot less marking!

Using the ideas

The lesson ideas which follow are not laid out to fit any particular lesson plan or scheme template as most schools have their own model. I am not restricting or dictating the learning objective for each idea, but I have suggested and identified key skills and opportunities for cross curricular work and some differentiation.

The lesson **ideas can be used in any order**, although some such as the advertising unit make sense to be followed in the order I have suggested. Some ideas are designed to run across several curriculum areas over a long time period, others are quick tasks which I would embed within a lesson as a direct stimulus for a writing task or discussion.

Some ideas have been explained in more detail than others, this is simply to provide more guidance to teachers who may be unfamiliar with using drama.

I have used all of the ideas which follow with students ranging from primary schools to adults on training courses. As in all lessons, differentiation is the key either in terms of the stimulus provided, support materials such as writing frames or the response which is accepted.

Feel free to photocopy the resources I have suggested or ignore them and create your own.

Terminology

The list below is not exhaustive, and you might argue un-necessary. In most situations, no one, especially the students care what names are given to certain dramatic conventions, but they can look impressive on a lesson plan and as I have used them in the resources which follow, it will help if you understand what I am talking about. GCSE students can be given the list and encouraged to use the terms.

Conscience Alley – *students speak in role as the teacher / other students walk past.*

Flashback / Flashforwards – *what happened immediately before or after the event / image.*

Forum Theatre – *students observe a group and can call out 'Stop!' The group freeze and listen to the improvement suggested by the person who called out, this person can replace the member of the group he/she is giving feedback to.*

Freeze Frame / Still Image / Tableaux – *students create a **statue** in the style of a photograph or statue capturing a moment frozen in time.*

Hot-Seating- *similar to **mantle of the expert**. A student literally sits at the front of the room (or similar) in the 'hot seat' in order to answer questions in role which are posed by the other members of the class. Less confident students can select someone to support them in this task. The supporting student cannot answer questions directly but can whisper suggestions to the person in the hot seat.*

Improvisation – *responding / reacting to a situation spontaneously.*

Mantle of the Expert – *taking on the role of the person who can provide answers to a situation / give information during a group drama.*

Point of Tension – *the moment any story is building towards, the **climax** point where the story can go one way or another.*

Mime – *acting without words.*

Polished Improvisation – *a short piece of prepared but unscripted drama. Students discuss what will happen, where people will stand, what they will say etc. Students have the opportunity to practice / rehearse and refine their work.*

Role Play – *acting as a character, pretending to be someone else and speaking, thinking, reacting and moving as that character.*

Role on the Wall – *creating a character by adding facts to an outline shape drawn on a large sheet or board, usually displayed on the wall.*

Teacher in Role – *the teacher takes part in the drama as a character.*

Thought Tracking – *students in a drama or freeze-frame tell the audience what their character is thinking / feeling.*

When I am 'acting' as **Teacher in Role**, I usually put on a jacket / pair of glasses, hold a clipboard etc. anything which acts a visual symbol to denote I am no longer *Mrs. Rix* the teacher, I am now **X** from the drama. Similarly, as soon as I take off the jacket or put down the board, I am once again Mrs. Rix the teacher.

As a way of recording progress / collecting the ever-required evidence of learning I use self-analysis record sheets after some lessons. An example of the template I use is with the lesson about persuasion.

Guy Fawkes

Divide the class into groups of either two, three or four students and give out GF Resource sheets 1ab and 2ab – see differentiation at the end.

Allow time to read the information.

Students highlight facts and opinions, using different colours.

Create a Role on the Wall

If you are artistic draw an outline of a stylised head and shoulders showing the familiar hat and long hair, if not simply add the name Guy Fawkes as a title.

Using the post-it notes, students are given a few minutes to write interesting facts about Guy Fawkes – this is a group activity. The notes are then brought to the front of the room and stuck inside the outline of the figure under the heading 'what we know.'

Repeat the above, this time collecting notes outside the outline and under the title, 'what we think.'

Discussion

Teacher reads the first set of notes. This is an opportunity for you as the teacher to remove any inappropriate comments which may have been added by any 'lively' members of the class if you have any! This is also the time to remove / group together the repetitions which are bound to occur. If you are using set one and set two resource sheets, (or if you have not given sheets a and b to each student) this is an opportunity for students to hear facts which might not have been on their information sheet.

Ask the class after presenting each point:

Is this a fact, or should this point be moved to the 'what we think' list?

Ask for an explanation to justify moving any points from one category to another.

Repeat the above using the points from 'what we think' group.

Return to the resource sheets and ask the students to identify the key points from the text.

Resources & Skills

You will need:
Resource sheets - Guy Fawkes 1ab & 2ab.
Highlighter pens – 2 colours.
Post-it notes / small squares of paper with blue tack.
Pens for students to write notes.
Large sheet of paper to display at front of classroom for **Role on the Wall**– a white board or similar can be used, but paper allows the notes etc to be cleared quickly, stored and used in subsequent sessions with minimal fuss.
Small white boards and pens / A4 paper.

Key Skills
Reading for information
Inference & Deduction
Fact & Opinion
Speaking & Listening
Group work
Empathy
Research

Discuss

Are some points considered more or less important by different groups / students?
If so, why?

As a class agree on the key facts and arrange in chronological order. Teacher (or a student) writes each point on a separate white board / sheet of A4. The points are displayed, either by using blue-tack or by asking students to hold the boards, at the front of the room.

Once everyone is happy with the points and the chronology, assign a number to each board then divide the class into groups.
Assign each group a number. The number corresponds to a key fact from the timeline. If there are ten key points, there should be ten groups.

It might be necessary to combine or split events to make more or less points, however, this provides another opportunity for discussion.

Explain

We are going to create a **still image** or **tableaux** to represent each key moment as if it were an illustration or a photograph in a book.

If the students are new to this way of working we need to model how to create the still image just as we would model a piece of writing or demonstrate how to perform a cartwheel!

For example: *if the key point is Guy becoming a Catholic I would ask, who would be present when guy decided to follow the Catholic faith? In my example I have decided his mother and stepfather, the Priest, one or two friends and of course Guy himself.*

- *Position one student as if he/she was Guy's friend on lookout duty, remind students how dangerous it was to be a Catholic. Ask the class to suggest how the volunteer should stand/ sit/ crouch...*
- *Now take a second student and ask where they think Guy's mother would stand. Again, ask the class for suggestions to refine how 'Guy's mother' should be positioned.*
- *Repeat for the other members of the image.*

Don't expect students who have been placed, to stand like statues while the scene is being built around them, invite them to contribute ideas, **but** once everyone has been assigned a position warn the group that on the count of three they must assume their pose and stand still.

Allow the class to see the image then give the command to relax.

Ask for feedback:

- Could we improve the way someone was standing?
- Are we happy with their facial expression?
- Do we think a character should be in a different place?

Ask the group to repeat the **tableaux** and ask again for feedback. This is non-threatening for the volunteers and criticism is not aimed at the students in the image. Remember, it was the teacher and the rest of the class who constructed the image.

*I always remind my students that any criticism **must** be **constructive** not **destructive**.*
*We laugh **with**, not **at**!*

Forum Theatre

Repeat the task one last time and ask for any final improvements while the group are showing the **still image**. Anyone who can offer a suggestion, either repositions or swaps places with the original volunteer and demonstrates their idea showing how the character should stand etc.
Now allow the class to return to their groups and create their own images.

Give students a set amount of time to devise their image. I usually allow no more than five minutes.

Accept there will be some noise.

At this point as teacher, step back and let them get on with it, there is nothing more off putting than having someone hovering while ideas are being generated.

After a minute give the class a time check. Do a wander around the room and offer any help you feel is appropriate.

Before the end of the time allowed give the class the opportunity to build their images and invite one member of each group to slip out of the picture and look at their image with a critical eye. They suggest changes to their group. Repeat if necessary.

Now ask the groups to create a **caption / title** for their work. Remind them this is a picture from a book or a photograph from a newspaper. The captions are written on the small white boards and displayed in front of the still images for all to see.

On the count of three all groups create their **still image**, hold for a few seconds then relax.

The constant repositioning or recreating of the image and relaxing can appear tedious when written down, but this allows students the opportunity to think about, discuss and refine their work. It also helps to break down any nerves.

Group One show their image along with their caption while the rest of the class observe. This group 'dissolves' and Group Two show their work and so on.

With a class who are new to drama I would stop at this point for a break.

Groups take up their **tableaux** positions again and the teacher introduces the idea of a **Conscience Alley**.

Eventually students are able to do this as you walk past or stand beside them, however, to introduce the convention tell each student that when you tap their shoulder they should speak, saying only a word or phrase as if they were the character they are representing. The words spoken can either be what their character might say or what they are thinking.

If we use the example from earlier, the student portraying the Priest might simply say, "Amen." The student on lookout might say, "I wish they would hurry up, I'm sure I heard someone!" because that is what the character is thinking.

If students are confident ask them to produce a short (no more than 30 seconds) **polished improvisation**. They should either begin by bringing their **still image** to life or use their **still image** as an end position.

Each group shares their work.

Split the class into groups and ask them to discuss Guy Fawkes.

For example:
- Reasons which might have caused Guy Fawkes to call himself Guido while he was abroad.
- People or situations which could have prompted him to become a Catholic.
- Events which could have led to his involvement in the gunpowder plot.
- Are students surprised by any of the points provided on sheets 1ab / 2ab?

Use the boards or sheets of paper with the captions as prompts, this is especially useful if this part of the project is taking place after a break of some kind.

Take feedback.

The Mantle of the Expert or Hot Seat characters

A volunteer (student or teacher) answers questions **in role**. The questions are asked by the other students as if they were journalists or investigators.
In order to give students a sense of ownership over the drama, ask who they think could / should be interviewed.

The list of characters could include:
- The shop keeper who sold the gunpowder.
- The landlord/lady who owned the property rented by the plotters.
- A neighbour who saw the men arrive for their meetings.
- The person who received the letter.
- Old school friends.

This activity can be done with one character answering the rest of the class or divide the class into groups and assign one **expert** to each group.

For example:
There could be one person who received the letter, or six. If you use the multiple character option, the journalists in each group will receive slightly different information which leads to a variation in the reports produced.

***Hot Seating** Guy Fawkes can produce some interesting responses. I will never forget the boy who, when asked who told him to blow up Parliament, answered: my conscience!*

Written Task

This can be done in class either individually or in pairs or after preparation in class the written work could be given as a homework task.

Using the information gathered from the **Hot Seating** exercise with the **experts**, create the newspaper front page announcing the attempt by the plotters to blow up Parliament.

Encourage the students to observe the usual conventions when producing a newspaper.

For example:
- Adverts could be created to promote shops selling firewood, sword sharpening etc.
- Sub-articles can be written to create other stories which might have been happening at the time, such as stories linked to the plague, 'celebrity' gossip etc.

Differentiation

The resource sheets are differentiated both in content and arrangement but can be discreetly handed out, so they appear to be similar.

More able students can be given both parts of resource sheet one.

Each student can be given a sheet or sheets. This ensures students listen to each other when they discuss the information, and it disguises the fact some students might have been given less to read than others.

Cut up the sheets and give groups / pairs a random assortment of facts.

The arrangement of groups can provide peer support, as can a supportive partner if hot seating is used.

The response and subsequent questioning by the teacher also provides an opportunity for personalised differentiation.

Some links to other curriculum areas / further literacy tasks

History – research life during 1600s.
R.E – religious tolerance, persecution of Catholics.
Geography – identify places in London, York, Spain.
Citizenship – the role of Parliament, our democratic state.
Art – wanted posters. Make quill pens. Firework patterns.
Diary writing in role as someone present at the time of the plot.
Letter writing.
Poetry inspired by fireworks.
Visit York.

Guido Fawkes

In 1568, Edith had given birth to a daughter named Anne, but the child died aged about seven weeks, in November that year. She bore two more children after Guy: Anne (1572), and Elizabeth (1575). Both were married, in 1599 and 1594, respectively.

Guy Fawkes was born in 1570 in York, the exact date is unknown, however, he was baptised at the church of St Michael le Belfrey on 16th April. It was the custom to baptise a child three days after birth, so he was probably born on 13th April. He was the second of four children born to Edward Fawkes and his wife, Edith.

Guy's parents were followers of the Protestant faith and were members of the Church of England, as were his paternal grandparents, however, his mother's family remained secret followers of the Catholic faith.

When he grew up, Guy Fawkes was described as being tall and muscular, with thick reddish-brown hair, a flowing moustache and a bushy reddish-brown beard.

In October 1591 Fawkes sold the estate that he had inherited. He travelled abroad and fought for Catholic Spain against Protestant rebels in the Spanish controlled Netherlands. Fawkes became a junior officer, and by 1603 had been recommended for promotion as a Captain. He travelled to Spain to seek support for a Catholic rebellion in England. He began using the Italian version of his name, Guido.

In 1604 James I publicly condemned Catholicism as a superstition, and he ordered all Catholic priests to leave England. Anyone refusing to attend Protestant services risked breaking the law and being fined, or worse!

The plotters purchased the lease to a room, it was unused and filthy, an ideal hiding place for the gunpowder the plotters planned to store. According to Guy Fawkes, twenty barrels of gunpowder were brought in at first, followed by sixteen more. The expected summer opening of Parliament was delayed until Tuesday, 5 November because of the threat of the plague. The delay caused much of the gunpowder to decay, so more was purchased, along with firewood to conceal it.

Under the plan, which was finalised in secret meetings during October, Fawkes was to light a fuse on November 5, 1605, during the opening of a new session of Parliament. James I, his eldest son, the House of Lords and the House of Commons would all be blown sky-high.

Resource 1b

By December 1604, the conspirators began tunnelling from their rented house to the House of Lords. During tunnelling, they heard a noise from the house above. Fawkes was sent out to investigate and returned with the news that the storage room above them, was being cleared out. It was directly beneath the House of Lords. The plotters decided to rent the room.

In 1579, when Guy was eight years old, his father died. Guy inherited an estate in Yorkshire and his own bed. His mother remarried several years later, to Denis Bainbridge. Bainbridge was a Catholic and he arranged for Guy to go to a school in York which was sympathetic to the Catholic faith. Guy became a Catholic.

After many failed attempts by English Catholics to assassinate James I, a plan was hatched in May 1604, by a small group of Catholic men: Thomas Percy, Jack Wright, Robert Catesby, Tom Wintour, and Guy Fawkes. They met at the Duck and Drake Inn in London, on Sunday 20th May 1604. At the meeting Catesby suggested a plan to blow up the Houses of Parliament with gunpowder. Afterward, all five men swore an oath of secrecy upon a prayer book. Eight other conspirators would later join what became known as the Gunpowder Plot. Catesby was the ringleader, but Fawkes is the most well-known member of the group.

A few of the conspirators were concerned about fellow Catholics who would be present at Parliament during the opening. Lord Monteagle received an anonymous letter warning him to stay away. The letter was shown to King James. The King ordered a search of the cellars underneath Parliament. Fawkes had taken up his station late on the previous night. He was found with matches and thirty-six barrels of gunpowder. He was arrested shortly after midnight.

While at school Guy became friends with brothers John and Christopher Wright, both became involved with the Gunpowder Plot. Other friends from school became priests, including Robert Middleton, who was executed for being a Catholic priest in 1601.

In June 1604 one of the conspirators, Thomas Percy, became a 'Gentleman Pensioner'. This role allowed him access to information as he was one of a group responsible for attending the Sovereign on State occasions. This position also allowed Percy to gain access to a house in London that belonged to John Whynniard, Keeper of the King's Wardrobe. Fawkes used the alias John Johnson, and he took a job as caretaker of a cellar—located just below the House of Lords—that the plotters had leased in order to stockpile gunpowder.

Guido Fawkes

Guy Fawkes was born in 1570 in York, he was baptised at the church of St Michael le Belfrey on 16th April. He was probably born on 13th April. He was the second of four children born to Edward Fawkes and his wife, Edith. His father was a Protestant. His mother's family remained secret followers of the Catholic faith.

In 1579, when Guy was eight years old, his father died. When his father died, Guy inherited an estate in Yorkshire and his own bed. His mother remarried several years later, to Denis Bainbridge. Bainbridge was a Catholic and he arranged for Guy to go to a school in York. which was sympathetic to the Catholic faith.

Guy became a Catholic. This might have been because of his stepfather's influence, his school (St Peter's in York) or the friends he met while at school.

While at school Guy became friends with brothers John and Christopher Wright, both were later involved with the Gunpowder Plot. Other friends from school became priests, including Robert Middleton, who was executed for being a Catholic priest in 1601.

When he grew up, Guy travelled and became a soldier. He fought on the side of the Spanish Catholics abroad. He began using the Italian version of his name, Guido.

When he grew up, Guy Fawkes was described as being tall and muscular, with thick reddish-brown hair, a flowing moustache and a bushy reddish-brown beard.

Thomas Percy, Jack Wright, Robert Catesby, Tom Wintour, and Guy Fawkes met at the Duck and Drake Inn in London, on Sunday 20th May 1604.

At the meeting Catesby suggested a plan to blow up the Houses of Parliament with gunpowder. Afterward, all five men swore an oath of secrecy upon a prayer book.

Guy Fawkes used the false name John Johnson. He took a job as caretaker of a cellar that the plotters had leased in order to stockpile gunpowder. It was located just below the House of Lords.

The plotters rented a room. It was unused and filthy. It was an ideal hiding place for the gunpowder.

Resource 2b

The opening of Parliament was delayed until Tuesday, 5 November because of the threat of the plague.

It was agreed that Guy Fawkes would light a fuse on November 5, 1605, during the opening of a new session of Parliament.

King James, his eldest son, the House of Lords and the House of Commons would all be blown sky high.

A few of the conspirators were concerned about fellow Catholics who would be present at Parliament during the opening.

Lord Monteagle received an anonymous letter warning him to stay away. The letter was shown to King James.

The King ordered a search of the cellars underneath Parliament. Guy Fawkes was found with matches and thirty-six barrels of gunpowder.

Advertising

Part 1

Class discussion: which adverts from television are most easily recognisable / memorable?

Why do they easily spring to mind?

- Slogan.
- Catch phrase.
- Recognisable action.
- Jingle.
- Celebrity endorsement.
- On going story.
- Humour.

Teacher creates a list of suggestions offered by the class. If examples are available, watch a few together.

Polished Improvisation

In groups, students create a short 30-60 second television advert for a product of their choice. The emphasis is on **improvisation** and students should not create a script. Students should create a **still image** to signify the end of their advert.

It is worth mentioning to students that the most successful humorous adverts, tend to be funny because the actors are not telling jokes.

I usually model an example with the help of four or five students.

I arrange four chairs very close together, two in front, two behind to represent a very small car.
My volunteer students over exaggerate opening car doors while struggling with their bags and making efforts to squeeze into the 'car' while I act as the voice over, asking the audience if they would like to enjoy more family days out etc. but feel restricted due to their tired old car.
The chairs are then pulled apart to create the impression of a larger vehicle and I extoll the virtues of the vehicle being advertised, as the family relax in comfort in the new car.
This works best if the tallest students are used to represent the children in my T.V family.

Allow approximately 5 minutes for preparation.
Give regular time checks.
At the end of the time allowed bring the class to a stop and on the count of three, every group has a dry run through from start to finish. This will be noisy.

Resources & Skills

You will need:
Part 1: Optional – examples of T.V. adverts to promote discussion.
Part 2: Examples of adverts from magazines, flyers / junk mail and television.
Paper, pencils, scissors, glue, rulers & card.
Access to research materials / internet.

Key Skills

Reading for information
Recognising & using the language of persuasion
Fact & Opinion
Speaking & Listening
Group work
Creativity
Decision Making
Problem Solving
Research
Vocabulary

As the groups 'rehearse' their adverts the teacher times their work. This allows each group the opportunity to determine whether their work is too long / short.

If students are confident each group can share their work. I usually follow each performance by asking named students who have been pre-warned, to give an example of one thing they particularly liked about the work they have just watched.

If your students are still unsure / reluctant to share their work in front of their peers, number each group and have half the class perform while the other half watch.

For example:
In a class with six groups, Group One is observed by Group Two. At the same time Group Three is observed by Group Four and Group Five is observed by Group Six. Feedback is given by the observers, then the second half of the class perform for their partner group.

Advertising Part 2

Revisit the list of successful advertising strategies from Part One.
Display the list.

Share out the examples of adverts from newspapers or magazines or display examples on the Interactive White Board. Students identify the strategies which have been used in the examples provided.

Divide the class into groups and either allocate or allow students to choose a product to promote.

Students work in groups to create an advertising campaign for their new product.

The campaign must include:
- An advert which will appear in a magazine / on the side of a bus / bill board.
- A television advert by way of a polished improvisation.

Each member of the group must contribute to the research and produce an example to appear in the magazine; this task should not be delegated to the most talented artist in the group.

Agree a time limit and let them get on with it!
The time allowed could be before the end of the lesson, if so allow time for presentations, or if the cross-curricular ideas below are incorporated, more time will be needed.

Differentiation

Differentiation will be by outcome and if groups are of mixed ability, peer support will allow all students the opportunity to contribute.

Differentiated support in research tasks will be needed.

Nets can be provided for the Mathematics and Design Technology tasks.

Some links to other curriculum areas / further literacy tasks

Art – posters and flyers to advertise the product. Story boards to explain the television advert. Create a brand feature / logo for the product.

Science – nutrition & healthy eating.

Mathematics & Design Technology – design and make a box for the product. Data collection & graph work via surveys/ customer research to find popular flavours, acceptable prices etc.

Music - compose a jingle.

I.T – research. Using the computer to create the work. Record / video the adverts.

The more adventurous could work with the kitchen staff or food technology department and actually make the product.

Students can collect the examples of adverts as homework tasks.

I used a variation of this lesson with a group of GCSE students. They had access to a variety of props which they were challenged to find alternative uses for. They then created the advertising campaign as above.

In a similar way another group of older students were told to find and repurpose anything they could find in the room. One group turned a roll of bin bags into a clothing brand and the project spiralled into a fashion show for clothing created from recycled items.

Peer Pressure

Part 1

Building belief in the drama is important, therefore do not skip the 'build up' in favour of diving into the main activity.

If possible, clear a space so students can sit on chairs in a circle. If this is not possible, adapt some of the activities to suit the space you are using.

In pairs students create a list of qualities which make a good friend.
Share with the class. Teacher compiles a class list of qualities to display.

Students find a partner and number themselves One and Two. They do not need to sit together; it can work better if at this stage they remain in different parts of the room. If they are sitting with their partner, students should arrange their chairs to sit back-to-back.

For the next part of the lesson, the teacher narrates a story line which the students **mime**:

- *Imagine you are home; you are reading an article about your favourite band or singer. Decide whether you are in the garden, your bedroom, the kitchen… and now decide how you are sitting. If you are in the kitchen, are you sitting at the table or leaning against a bench? Sit or stand (or lie) as you imagine yourself. **Move into position silently**.*

- *Now decide how you are reading the article. Is it in a magazine? Is it on your phone? Perhaps you are sitting at a desk using a computer. Alter your position to make it clear and on the count of three freeze.*

- *As I move the story on, I want you to act out the story. You can move and react, but you must remain silent. You can **mime** a shout, or a cheer.*

- *You read the article carefully. Suddenly, a paragraph catches your attention! You read it again.*

- *The paragraph you are particularly interested in is a competition. First prize is an opportunity to meet your favourite pop star(s). You decide to enter the competition. **Show without speaking how you do this:** perhaps you use a pen to fill in an entry form in the magazine which you then cut out and put into an envelope; perhaps you follow a link on-line and tap out a response on your computer/phone/tablet…*

- *Several weeks pass and you forget about the competition. Then, you receive a reply. Decide how the competition organisers contact you. Do they send an email, a message, a letter or do they telephone?*

- *When you have decided, fold your arms as a signal to me. On the count of three, and **still without speaking to your partner,** you are going to move into a position and freeze. This position is to show how you reacted when you received the news about the competition. Anyone looking at your **still image** should be able to tell at a glance how you were contacted and whether or not you were successful.*

  Number One – Congratulations, you have won!
  Number Two - sorry, you were unsuccessful, but thank you for entering. Better luck next time.

Allow students time to create their individual images. Divide the room and allow half the class to look at their peers, then swap.

Thought Tracking

While half the class are in role and the other half are observing ask some students to explain how they are feeling using one word or a short phrase.

Improvisation

Ask for a volunteer pair to create an improvisation showing person number one telling person number two the good news:

  Number One has won a pair of front row tickets for the concert and a chance to go back stage and meet the band / singer. Number One will invite their partner to take the second ticket and go with them.

After watching the example, the class work in their pairs to produce their own **Polished Improvisations** based on Number One winning the competition.

The pairs decide themselves:
- Does Number One invite their partner immediately to take the second ticket?
- Does Number Two have to persuade their friend to take them rather than someone else?

Share some examples of the **Polished Improvisations**.

The students find a space slightly away from their partner.
Students **mime** preparing to go out: drying hair, make-up etc. Don't allow this to drag, this part is simply to build tension.

Explain

Both friends were very excited until finally the day of the concert arrives. You have arranged to meet in town. Just as you are about to head off or enter the venue one of you notices that your friend is wearing odd shoes.

There is no time to go home. What do you do?

In pairs, prepare a **Polished Improvisation** showing what happens when you meet and what happens next.

As teacher it is your choice to decide which friend is wearing the odd shoes or allow the students to decide.

Peer Pressure Part 2

Using the list of friendship qualities from last lesson, and the persuasive tactics employed by friends trying to convince their friend to attend the concert in odd shoes, generate a discussion about other things we are persuaded to do / persuade others to do for us.

For example:
- Stay out later than a parent is happy with.
- Attend a party.
- Try alcohol / cigarettes /drugs.
- Complete homework.
- Steal.

The suggestions will be age dependant, with older students suggesting more risqué ideas while younger children will suggest staying up past bedtime.

The discussion is to generate a variety of ideas and eliminate surprises when the students move to produce polished improvisations. On more than one occasion a student has used this lesson as a way of raising a safeguarding issue.

Students work in groups to produce a **polished improvisation** illustrating peer pressure.

After each group has shared their work hold a discussion.
- Was the persuasive tactic successful? Why?
- Do you agree with the outcome?
- Was the person right to succumb / ignore the persuasion? Why?

A variation is to look at family members using and responding to persuasion.
For example:
- Taking the blame for something a sibling has done.
- A child persuading a parent to extend a curfew.
- Persuading a parent to buy something.

Differentiation

This is achieved by the organisation of groups and pairs to ensure positive group dynamics and appropriate peer support.

Teacher questioning.

Self-Analysis sheets.

Some links to other curriculum areas / literacy tasks

PHSE - work surrounding relationships (age appropriate), bullying, peer pressure, 'staying safe.'

Adverts to announce / promote the competition in Part 1.

Careers – complete a personal skills development wheel, (there are dozens on-line) and use this to consider future development or career paths.

Art / Design Technology – design a pair of shoes.

Plan & Organise a concert with the Music Department, or a performance with the Drama Club, or a School Disco.

Self-Analysis Sheet 1

Name

Date

Lesson title

Self-Analysis Sheet 1(Alternative)

Three Stars and a Wish…

Self-Analysis Sheet 2

Name:

Date:

Lesson Title:

Today I worked with

My contribution to the work was to…

I am pleased with…

My work could have been made better if…

Next time I will try to…

Self-Analysis Sheet 3

Name:

Date:

Lesson Title:

Write a brief explanation of today's lesson and the contribution you made.

Are you pleased with the work you produced? Explain why.

How could your work be improved? Future targets…

Conflict

Part 1
Introduce the idea of stereotypes.
Hand out cards with character titles. Students must not share what is written on their card.

Whole class or one section of the room at a time, stand up and on the count of three, assume a pose which they believe represents or illustrates the character from their card.

Discuss
How did we identify the old person / teacher, etc.? Discuss the use of body language to infer and emphasise meaning. Remind students that body language, including facial expression, and tone of voice are important when conveying meaning.

If possible arrange the students in a circle, this is not essential, but it makes the following activity easier.

How many ways can we use / express the word 'Yes'?

For Example:
- Firmly such as a parent insisting it is bedtime.
- A teacher confirming an answer which has been offered.
- Agreeing to a marriage proposal.
- Excitedly or reluctantly...

Students stand in a circle and one by one give an example and demonstrate different ways to use the word 'yes.'

Repeat using the word 'no.'

Check the class have a common understanding of 'conflict' and 'resolution.'

Working with a partner students consider situations where there could be some conflict and a barrier.

For example:
- A game of tennis the net is the barrier.
- Neighbours arguing, the garden fence is the barrier.
- Someone is given the wrong change in a shop / bar, the counter is the barrier.

Resources & Skills

You will need:
Character title cards.
Self-Analysis sheets.

Key Skills

Time Management
Verbal & Non-verbal communication
Creativity
Co-operation
Decision Making
Confidence

The pairs are given a set amount of time to prepare a **polished improvisation**, showing a conflict where there is a barrier separating the people involved in the dispute.
Students are only allowed to use the words 'Yes' and 'No.'

As an audience we should be able to identify:
- The relationship between the characters.
- The cause of the conflict.
- The barrier.
- How / if, the conflict is resolved.

Share work and discuss the bullet points.

Differentiation

Choice of character card.

Peer support / challenge in assignment of partners.

If the class are new to the concept of **polished improvisations**, or lack confidence, the teacher should model an example with a student.

Links to other curriculum areas / literacy tasks.

Write a letter of complaint / apology.

Humanities – World conflict.

Citizenship – Local issues which generate conflict such as development plans, the state of the roads, local services.

PHSE – Look at ways to resolve conflict with families and friendship groups. Discuss bullying and create posters showing how conflict between friends can be resolved to prevent bullying.

An old person	A teacher	A goal keeper	A swimmer
A parent	A bully	Someone who is frightened.	You have just lost £1,000.
A man	A woman	Someone thinking.	Someone in love

The Village Conflict

Conflict Part 2

The Village

As a teacher, I loved using a long running drama which spanned several lessons. The opportunity to develop other curriculum areas and to find real reasons to write, made planning a doddle and eased the burden of marking! The drama can be picked up / left as and when appropriate. I strongly recommend familiarising yourself with this lesson and doing some preparation before beginning.

There are some elements of this drama which will be controlled by the students, however, as the teacher it is your responsibility to ensure the drama moves in the correct direction towards the desired points of conflict.

Display the large sheet of paper where everyone can see it. Using the marker pens create a simple map. I usually draw something to represent hills, a river and a wood. This can be prepared in advance, or drawn as the class watches.
Add a main road across the bottom of the sheet.

> **Resources & Skills**
>
> **You will need:**
> A large sheet of paper.
> Marker pens.
> Post-it notes (optional).
> Cards in two distinct colours.
> A clipboard.
>
> **Key Skills**
> Verbal & Non-verbal communication.
> Creativity.
> Co-operation.
> Research
> Decision Making.
> Confidence.

Explain

We are creating a 'perfect' or as near as possible, perfect village.

Create a list of desirable features but do not add them to the 'map' yet. Students make suggestions and teacher records the features, creating a list.
Alternatively, use the post-it notes and students display ideas, creating a **Role on the Wall**. The role is the Village.

Remember your aim is to create a low pollution, desirable place to live, your responsibility at this point is to steer students away from adding features such as a shopping precinct. Use the idea of the main road as a link to a large town or city where you can locate features which you want to avoid, at least to begin with.

Examples of features:
- A village shop.
- A village green and sports pavilion.
- A church.
- A school.

- A pub.
- A coffee shop.
- A caravan site.
- A post-office.
- A picnic spot.

Encourage the students to think about adding details to the suggested features. Is there a nature reserve near the river? Is there a bridge or a pond?

Take suggestions but retain discreet control as **you** place the features on the map. Include a couple of roads running through the village and discuss the best place to position bus stops and foot paths.

Move on to deciding where to position the communal features such as the school.

Tell the students they are going to mark where they live on the map. This might require more roads / lanes.

Select one of the communal features such as the school. Ask who would like to be the teacher(s) and take the opportunity if necessary to explain the difference between small country schools with few pupils and only a couple of teachers and larger schools in towns. Select a teacher and allow him / her to mark where they live on the map with an **X** and their initials.

Continue to mark the other communal features from the list and try to determine some roles. **Do this before filling the village with houses not linked to the features.**

For example:
If student A suggested the village shop, tell them they own that business. Now ask if they live above the business or elsewhere in the village. If they live elsewhere the student marks the position of their home on the map.
Invite student B to come to the map. This student suggested having a coffee shop. This student is now the owner of the coffee shop…

When the features which require 'ownership' have been allocated you should have a group of students who have a role (employer / business owner) and a larger group of students who have yet to be assigned a position / role. The latter of these two groups now mark their homes on the map.

Later invite the students to draw boxes around the initials to illustrate large, detached properties, rows of terraced houses etc. This adds to a sense of ownership and reality.

The map should be displayed throughout the drama and all associated lessons.

Writing in Role
- The owners of the businesses create an advert to advertise for staff.
   Students can work alone or with another business owner.
- The remaining group of students write letters applying for the positions.

Arrange the letters of application with the appropriate advert.

Peer review

Which letters / positions seem most appealing? Why?

Create a display using the adverts.

Hot Seating

Students have short interviews to apply for the jobs. It is important at this point that positions are not awarded based on friendship / popularity.

Polished Improvisation

In pairs or groups of three or four prepare a short, **polished improvisation** where one student is telling the rest of their group about their day.

For example:

- Was the interview successful? Did the student employ someone/ get the job?
- How do they feel? Are they worried about paying the bills, excited, relieved, resentful?
- Where is the drama taking place? Is this a family conversation at home, a meeting with friends in the pub or while fishing?

Show each of the Polished Improvisations.

There should now be a group of students who are employed / business owners and a group of students who are unemployed. Give this last group of students a coloured card. I am going to assume the colours red, and green have been used.

The **Green Group** are wealthy. They all have careers in the large town / city. These students can now decide whether they live full time in the village or whether they only stay in the village during weekends and holidays.

The **Red Group** have always lived in the village. They do not have jobs in the city, they remain unemployed.

This division will begin to create an undercurrent of tension.

The tension can be increased by giving *some* of the houses which belong to the **Red Group** to students from the Green Group or to a business owner, or to the character mentioned below, thus changing the status of some students from homeowner to tenant.

Choose a student to be a wealthy landowner. They can be a farmer or a 'Lord / Lady of the Manor' character. Allow them to move house and mark off a large section of the map to denote land owned by this person. Include a large area near the village, several houses in the village and land extending up to and into the village. This decision is made by the teacher. I usually give an area near the caravan site if there is one and allow the village green to be owned by this character. Businesses within the designated areas can be owned by or leased from the new character. This adds more tension.

Build the Village

Students of all ages seem to enjoy this task. Students make models of their homes and / or businesses. Determine an area for display and ensure a realistic scale, there is always someone who wants to make a tiny cottage out of an old shoe box while the rest of the village is the size of single portion cereal cartons.

This makes a good homework task with older students and even GCSE students enjoy the creativity of the task. As the models are completed create a display. As teacher you will need to provide a space and create the other features such as the river etc.
Sawdust mixed with paint produces excellent grass and sticks to most surfaces without glue. Sponges dipped in paint make realistic bushes and twigs stuck into plasticine make great trees...
If you intend to use this lesson more than once the basic environment can be prepared on a board and stored for future use.

As individuals / pairs / groups students create a **tableaux** to show a typical moment in their daily life. This helps to **Build Belief** in the drama.

For example:
- Serving in the café.
- Meeting friends for coffee.
- Arguing about bills.
- Fishing in the river...

Once the **still images** have been organised, bring the village to life with each image simultaneously melting into spontaneous **improvisation** until told to freeze by the teacher. This will be noisy.

Conscience Alley
You should then take a stroll around the village with each **still image** coming to life, speaking or moving in role until you have moved past the group.

Now that we have a flavour for daily life in the village introduce an element of tension by starting a rumour or spreading gossip. This can easily be achieved by:

- **Narrating** the story.
- Using the **Mantle of the Expert**. Quietly instructing a student to start a specific rumour.
- **Teacher in Role**. Grab a clip board and wait for the class to respond.

Use one of the conventions mentioned above to introduce the gossip:
People in smart clothes and carrying clip boards have been seen wandering around the village.
Who are they?
What do they want?

In their groups students discuss the rumours.
Use **polished improvisations** to share the villager's thoughts about the strangers.
Ask the villagers what they would like to do?

For example:
- Hold a village meeting.
- Interview someone. Who?
- Hold a protest. Why? What kind of protest? How will it be organised? Who will be in charge?

From this point follow the direction the students dictate.
If they want a meeting in the Village Hall to find out who the strangers are and what they want, turn your classroom or workspace into the Village Hall.

Let the students decide:
- How will the chairs be arranged?
- Who will sit where?
- Who is in charge?

If they want to hold a protest, allow them to make signs and banners. Those not in favour of the protest can be interviewed by T.V or news journalists...

Once the strangers and their purpose in the Village has been discovered explore the conflict which is then created within families / between neighbours / friends etc.

Ensure the conflict is demonstrated by using **improvisations and polished improvisations**.

Direct the drama towards one of the suggested narratives which follow.

Narrative Suggestions

1. **Development of the Pub**

The owner has agreed to buy some land from the wealthy land owner. The land is adjacent to the pub and the owner intends to add a fancy restaurant and bedrooms as well as a leisure complex.
This will create a split within the village.

Those in favour might include:
- The land owner who stands to benefit financially.
- Some unemployed villagers hoping to find work.
- The Green Group who can afford to use the new facilities.
- Business owners who hope to profit from the development.

Those against might include:
- Café / coffee shop who will lose business.
- Anyone owning a B & B.
- The Red Group who cannot afford to use the new facilities.
- People worried about extra noise / traffic.

2. **The Recycling Plant / Waste Processing Centre**

The wealthy landowner has agreed to sell some land in or close to the village. A large company are going to develop the site.
This will create a split within the village.

Those in favour might include:
- The land owner who stands to benefit financially.
- Some unemployed villagers hoping to find work.
- Some business owners who might make money by selling food and drink to the construction workers.

Those against might include:
- Café / coffee shop who might lose business from locals.
- Anyone owning a B & B or the caravan site: who wants a holiday next to a smelly waste site?
- Environmental groups.
- People worried about extra noise / traffic.

3. An Outdoor Adventure Development

The wealthy landowner has agreed to sell some land in or close to the village. A large company are going to develop the site, adding large carparks, fast food outlets and activities such as zip-lining, paintball etc.
This will create a split within the village.

Those in favour might include:
- The land owner who stands to benefit financially.
- Some unemployed villagers hoping to find work.
- Some business owners who might make money by the visitors coming to the attraction.
- People wanting to use the new facilities.

Those against might include:
- Café / coffee shop who might lose business.
- People living close to the new site.
- Environmental groups.
- People worried about extra noise / traffic.

A similar drama focussing on conflict can be developed by creating a **factory** or place of work rather than the village. Belief in the drama is established by creating a simple production line of box assembly staff, box fillers, staff taping the boxes shut and those lifting them from one place to another.

Use Conscience Alley down the production line to establish belief in the roles of the students as workers.
Uses still images and **polished improvisation** showing daily life at work and at home when the working day has ended.
Rather than a land owner, create a factory owner and promote managers / foreman.
In the Village, conflict was introduced by dividing the students into business owners and members of the Red or Green Group, introduce a level of conflict in the factory by docking pay from half the group for poor work and give a bonus to other workers.

Use strangers to create rumours. Will the factory be sold? Are jobs safe? Spread rumours of redundancy / promotion opportunities.

Encourage workers to spy on colleagues and report those not working hard / speaking ill of the company...

Introduce a Trade Union Rep. Will the workers strike? What happens within families / friendships where someone is promoted, and someone wants to strike?

Differentiation

Writing templates can be used for the written tasks.

Allocation of roles.

In whole class drama situations, the teacher can stand close to students lacking confidence and offer confirmation and support or discreetly make suggestions.

Links to other curriculum areas / literacy tasks

I.T - Use of computer to research skills / wages etc. for the job vacancies. Letters can be written using computers.

Geography / mapping – features of towns, villages etc. Reading and using symbols. Urbanisation. Create personal maps of the village.

Mathematics – grid references. Scale.

Design Technology – make a scale model of houses / buildings in the village.

Art – designing the village. Posters.

Science – environmental issues. Pollution.

Social Science – Democracy. The rights of individuals. Morals / ethics/ economics.

Letter writing. Newspaper articles. Diary entries written in role.

Debate – how do we protest peacefully?

Using a Stimulus

Resources & Skills

You will need:
Old theatre posters.
Or, leaflets or flyers
advertising a play or theatre
production.

Key Skills
Time Management
Creativity
Co-operation
Decision Making
Confidence
Vocabulary
Inferential reading
Team Work

The breakdown of marks awarded by exam boards varies but in some instances students can be awarded up to 40% of their GCSE marks for their performance inspired by a stimulus.
This stimulus could be a letter, a photograph, a piece of music, a hat, in fact, almost anything!
The same type of stimulus is equally useful in any drama lesson.

Posters

Using a Stimulus i.

Display a poster at the front of the room. Most theatres will happily give away old posters at little or no cost. Less well-known performances such as a play rather than a popular musical work best, this avoids students being influenced by the story they already know.

Teacher acts as scribe to write down lists of things we know, things we assume and questions we would like to have answered, based on the visual clues provided by the poster.

For example:
A poster advertising 'Long Day's Journey Into Night' depicting a lone house with the beach in the background might prompt the following:
We know a house is part of the story. It is at the beach.
We assume something has happened in the house.
We want to know who lives in the house. What has happened to the people?
Use the text. Have the occupants undertaken a long journey as refugees or fundraisers? The date might be used to tell us when something happened.

A poster for 'Death of a Salesman' shows a door-to-door salesman holding heavy bags.
We know a salesman is involved.
We assume something has happened to the man. The words suggest he died; we assume this happened while he was working.
We want to know how he died, if there was an accident or if it was deliberate...

Make the list of things we know, assume and want to know, as extensive and creative as possible.
Remember we are not second guessing what the play is about. We are using the information provided by the poster.

Polished Improvisation

In groups students prepare a ninety second **polished improvisation** in the style of a television news bulletin based on the poster and using the information generated by the lists which have been created. There should be a news anchor in the studio, a reporter at the scene and one or more witnesses. The poster will be displayed behind the studio anchor person as a visual clue to the audience in the same way that each news article has a picture behind the person in the studio.

Remind students that a news bulletin aims to provide viewers with:

- Who?
- What?
- Where?
- When?
- How?
- Sensational language is used to grip the audience.
- The bulletin should last 90 seconds.

As the groups prepare, give time checks and provide the opportunity to run through their work against a ninety second timer.

Groups show their work.

Differentiation

Some students will need help to stay focussed on the inferential information in the images and might need more support to avoid a re-telling of the actual play being advertised.

Some students will benefit from watching examples of news broadcasts before preparing their own.

Challenge can be added by providing different posters for each group. The less able can use the poster which has been seen and discussed by the class. More able students can be given an unseen poster.

Links to other curriculum areas /literacy tasks

This is very open ended as so much depends upon your choice of poster. The poster from my example 'Long Day's journey...' could link to geography and examine coastal erosion...

Newspaper articles to support the television news broadcast.

Diary entries written by characters involved in the drama. For example: the Salesman might have written about his concerns; was he being threatened, followed, blackmailed?

The language conventions used by the news reporters and witnesses can be analysed.
Older students can link their own work to a deeper analysis of language, considering the use of Standard English, leading questions and political bias.

Compare television news reports with those from newspapers or the internet.

Use cameras or tablets to record the news broadcasts.

Art: Photographs / Paintings / Music

Resources & Skills

You will need:
Photographs.
A painting or image.
Any items to use as a visual prop.
Music.

Key Skills

Time Management
Verbal and Non-verbal communication
Creativity
Co-operation
Decision Making
Confidence
Inferential reading
Speaking and Listening

Using a Stimulus ii.

For students who are familiar with drama, this lesson is a doddle, provided you choose appropriate photographs or paintings.

Photographs and prints of paintings can be copied and given to students or shown to the class using a large screen or interactive white board.

I do not provide any information relating to the picture / photograph. The aim is for students to use their imagination, not test their historical knowledge or their awareness of current events, although these areas can be explored later as cross-curricular activities.

Students work in groups to recreate the image then produce a **polished improvisation** showing either what they think happened immediately before or after the photograph was taken.

There should be a **tableaux** to bookmark the beginning and the end of the **improvisation**. Remember, the still image is showing a moment captured in time rather than a posed arrangement for the camera.

Hot Seat the members of each group while they are in the positions at the end of their polished improvisation.

- How are they feeling?
- Why are they there?
- What are they hoping will happen?

'The Scream' by Edvard Munch is always well received and using the simple format described above, produced some excellent results with a GCSE group.

As an alternative to a visual prompt, a piece of music can be used.

Play the piece and when invited, students offer a word or short phrase to explain how the music made them feel.

Still images and **polished improvisations** are prepared based around the suggestions offered by the students.

If you have access to a drama studio, play the music in darkness to eliminate distractions then allow students to experiment using different lights and colour themes to enhance their work.

Differentiation

This is achieved by subtle acceptance / challenge regarding responses made by students.

Discreet dissemination of different photographs or prints. Provide questions with the images to encourage students the look at details.

Provide a vocabulary list to help students using music as a stimulus.

Links to other curriculum areas /literacy tasks

Use the ideas generated for creative writing.

Humanities – research issues surrounding the subject matter illustrated in the photographs and paintings. Explore the history and culture reflected in the images.

Art – research the artist who painted the picture used as a stimulus. Create own work in the style of the artist. Create a visual response to the music.

Music – produce own compositions to contrast the mood of the stimulus piece / in the style of the stimulus music or as a response to a painting which has been used.

PHSE – produce a mood board.

Poetry

Using a Stimulus iii.

Divide the class into groups and give each group an envelope containing the cut-up poem.
Do not include the title.

Use a paper cutter to break up the poem or some students will piece it together jig-saw style.

Working in groups / pairs students put the poem together in an order which they think makes sense. Use the blue tack to secure the pieces into the chosen order.

Alternatively, give each group a stanza and ask what they think the poem is about.

Share and discuss the different responses.

At this point you can choose to either continue with the versions of the poem created by the groups or hand out copies of the original.

Using whichever version of the poem you have decided to continue with, students decide:
- Which characters are in the poem.
- Where the narrative is taking place.

Students should be ready to justify their answers to the questions, but also accept responses from their peers which may be very different to their own ideas, especially if different versions of the poem are being used.

Groups create a **tableaux**. Use one key line from the poem as a title for the image.

Using the highlighter pens, student identify lines / phrases / words which would be spoken by the characters they believe are in the poem or section of poem they have been given.

Once the lines have been colour-coded, students should add brief annotations to remind them how they think the lines would be spoken / delivered. This effectively creates a script and is one of the few times I use scripted work in a drama lesson.

In groups, students prepare a **polished improvisation** incorporating the 'scripts' they have created.

You will need:

Copies of your selected poem for each group. One copy should be the original, complete text and one should be cut up into separate stanzas.

Envelopes.
Blue tack.

Highlighter pens in a range of colours for each group.

Key Skills

Verbal and Non-verbal communication
Creativity
Co-operation
Decision Making
Confidence
Inferential reading
Speaking and Listening
Problem Solving
Empathy

If using the original version of the poem, show the work of each group in the order dictated by the poem.

Differentiation

Provide illustrations / photographs to support less able students and give them shorter pieces of text.

More able students can be given more complex / lengthier text or provide them with a poem which has been cut into more pieces.

Allow students to colour-code a stanza rather than the entire poem.

Challenge can be added by allowing students to add more dialogue during the polished improvisations, but the lines from the poem must be included. Encourage students to play around with the text and perhaps divide a phrase to enable more than one character to deliver parts of one verse, regardless of punctuation. How does this change the drama?

Links to other curriculum areas /literacy tasks

Study the chosen poem in more detail with the context provided.

Look at other work by the poet, or poems about the same subject matter / theme written by other poets.

Write poetry and use the poems written by the class to create drama.

Humanities – work associated with the cultural and political / religious context of the selected poem.

Write diary entries / newspaper reports etc. in role.

Props.

Using a Stimulus iv.

You will need:
An item of your choice.

Part 1

Key Skills

An easy and very quick lesson can be arranged with limited planning or resources, using physical props. This type of lesson is handy if there is an unexpected timetable change, or a cover lesson is needed with little notice.

Verbal and Non-verbal communication
Creativity
Co-operation
Decision Making
Confidence
Speaking and Listening
Problem Solving

An item (literally anything) is placed on a table or if space allows, sit the students in a circle and place the object in the centre of the circle.

Give students the opportunity to look at the item and invite suggestions to answer:
- What could this be used for?
- Who does /did the item belong to?

Try to move away from the obvious answers and encourage students to be creative, looking for alternative and imaginative uses for the object.

Props such as a hat, a clock, a ball of string... basically any item you can get your hands on will work, unusual items which students are unfamiliar with can provide interesting results. Paintings can be displayed on a large screen, but copies of photographs or prints of paintings which can be handled allow the students to make closer inspection of details, this also means different groups can work using different images. When using physical props, it is important to give students the opportunity to handle them.

Allow students to enter the circle to closely examine and demonstrate using the object.

As students suggest various ways in which the item can be used, other students can enter the circle, interact with the person already there and either support / develop the same way of using the prop or move into using the item in a completely different way.

For example:
Student A picks up the item which is a mug. The student mimes filling the mug with water from a tap and uses the mug to water a plant. Student B enters, admires the plant and takes the mug. Student A leaves the circle and student B uses the mug as a telephone. Student C enters the circle and responds to the phone call. Student B hands over the mug and Student C mimes being caught in a rain storm and the mug becomes an umbrella.

Working in pairs or small groups, students create short **improvisations** or **polished improvisations,** based on creative and imaginative ways to use the prop.

Differentiation

Provide a range of objects and allocate or allow students to choose which object to use.

Links to other curriculum areas /literacy tasks

Art – use the objects for still life drawing.

Science – recycling. Look at the environmental impact of the objects. Are they still used / manufactured? What type of carbon footprint do they create? Can the objects be repurposed?

Design Technology – design a machine or gadget to perform a task or a chore. Look at the development of technology over the last twenty, fifty or one hundred years.

Props. Part 2

Arrange the coat either draped on or over a chair before the students arrive.

As **teacher in role**, ask if anyone owns the coat /knows who it belongs to…

Empty the pockets and share the contents.

Discuss:
- who do we think owned the coat?
- What is the significance of the items in the pockets of the coat?
- What do we think has happened to the owner?

Ask students who, apart from the owner, could we talk to?

For example:
- Someone from the bus station.
- Someone from the local shops.

What would we like to ask these characters?
Either select students to be **Hot Seated** in role or take on the roles yourself.

From this point it is difficult to predict the next steps because so much will be determined by the characters the students choose to question, and what they choose to ask.

Suggested activities:
- A whole class drama to investigate the disappearance of the owner of the coat.
- Diary writing in role as the coat owner.
- A news broadcast relating to the disappearance of the person.
- Polished improvisations in groups showing what happened before the person disappeared.

The key to success is to remind the students about the items in the pockets and question their meaning / significance.

An alternative way to introduce this lesson is to draw a chalk outline of a figure as in a crime scene, or mark one with masking tape.
Chalk can be more difficult than you might imagine to remove from certain types of carpet!

You will need:

A coat with pockets, ideally not one the students have seen you wearing.

Items to put in the pockets: Keys, analogue watch, library card, loose change, a basic shopping list, a bus ticket, a locket or photograph in a wallet or similar…
   If the above items cannot be found see alternative method of preparation at the end of this section.

Key Skills
Creativity
Co-operation
Decision Making
Speaking and Listening
Problem Solving
Confidence
Critical thinking
Empathy
Social skills

If you are unable to lay your hands on the required items, print and laminate some images and lay them around the outline of the figure or around the coat.

You can go into as much depth and detail as you feel necessary in setting up this lesson and either stop after a single lesson or run the theme over several lessons. However, a note of warning, I once went a step beyond the abandoned coat and made a figure by adding trousers, boots, a hat over a wig, having stuffed the garments with newspaper it looked very realistic but terrified one of the more sensitive members of the class. A few years later a very obliging teaching assistant dressed up as the 'figure' and the realism of the 'body' elicited several parental letters of concern!

Differentiation

This is determined by the age and maturity of the students.

Laminated pictures of the items can have points of interest or additional support information printed on the back.

Increase the level of challenge by using questions to promote deeper thinking. These can be printed along with the images.

Links to other curriculum areas /literacy tasks

Newspaper reports relating to the found jacket / body.

Art – still life drawing of the jacket.

PHSE – vulnerability, loneliness, mental health.

Discuss how we use stereotypes and preconceptions to make quick judgements based on appearances. How different would our drama have been if the jacket or contents of the pockets had been different?

Legends

Poetry is one of my favoured forms of inspiring a drama, but stories and legends can be used in the same way.

The following idea uses the legend of The Mistletoe Bough, a story which has been popular since the early 1800s.

Explain

Our drama is set about two hundred years ago and our work space is a large manor house / castle. There is going to be a very grand society party to celebrate a wedding.

- What would the setting / venue be like?
    Large.
    Shadowy corners.
    Heavy furniture.
    Wall hangings...

- Who would be present?
    The Groom.
    The Bride.
    Family members.
    Friends.
    Servants.

- What would everyone be doing?

Students choose **roles** but do not allow anyone to be the Bride or the Groom. Give students a few moments to decide where they are and what they are doing.

Some characters will be friends of the Bride / Groom they might believe in the fairytale romance or be concerned. Perhaps they expected the Bride to marry someone else...

Servants will be excited or might be moaning about the fussy guests and extra work, they might be whispering, passing on gossip about the Bride and Groom...

At a given signal, (I usually count down from three) the scene comes to life with everyone in role interacting with each other.

For example:
- A servant might be circulating among the guests offering drinks.
- Small groups of guests might be chatting and anticipating the arrival of the Bride or speculating about the Bride's dress.

Resources & Skills

You will need:

A large sheet of paper to record and display ideas. Character cards for the extension.

Key Skills
Creativity
Co-operation
Decision Making
Speaking and Listening
Problem Solving
Verbal and Non-verbal communication
Confidence
Critical thinking
Empathy
Social skills

44

- Some guests might be bored with the wait and be grumbling.

Remind students that their body language and manner of talking should help signify their role / character to the rest of us.

As **Teacher in Role**, begin a rumour and create speculation:

The Groom is significantly older than the Bride, this is his second marriage. Is the Bride in love, or after the Groom's substantial fortune? What happened to the first wife, divorce was not an option in those days?

Step out of role to instruct the students.

In small groups / clusters improvise conversations about the wedding. These conversations will be shared using a **Conscience Alley.**

As **Teacher in Role,** you will hover close to or join a group, when this happens the students should begin their conversation and become quiet as the teacher's character leaves.

Walk slowly from one group to another, pausing to 'eavesdrop' before moving on. If a group are struggling use your position within the group to ask questions **in role.**

*This **Conscience Alley** increases belief in the drama and allows the teacher to gauge how much / little direction is needed to move towards a point of suspicion and conflict.*

Once each group has participated remove yourself from the drama to narrate the next part of the story. You can either instruct the students to relax and allow them to step out of role or ask them to freeze and listen while still in role.

Explain

The wedding ceremony was held in the castle / manor house and although the Bride was a few minutes late, everything during the ceremony, appeared to go as planned. Some people seemed to think the Bride glanced towards the back of the hall once or twice but that was probably just because she was looking towards her friends. After the ceremony there was a feast.

The Bride seemed to grow bored. Remember she was much younger than her new husband. He wanted to talk (probably about business) with his friends, she was anxious to start dancing and having fun with her own much younger friends.

The Bridegroom was anxious to please his new Bride, so he happily encouraged her to go with her friends to have fun.

The younger members of the wedding party left the Grand Hall, and the Bride suggested a game of Hide and Seek.

At some point it may be worth discussing cultural / historical attitudes to marriage and the accepted age at which people were married. Juliet was twelve or thirteen and her parents were actively searching for a husband. Romeo was somewhere between sixteen and twenty-one.

Sometime later it was announced that it was time for the happy couple to cut the wedding cake and a servant was sent to bring the Bride and her young friends back to the Hall. However, the servant was unable to find the Bride. In fact, she was never seen again.

What happened?

In groups students create a **tableaux** to show what their characters were doing when everyone began to search for the Bride. Either use **Thought Tracking** or **Conscience Alley** to share information and move the story on.

Characters might:
- Be servants searching.
- Guests / friends searching.
- Some characters might be angry / worried.
- Some characters might be gossiping.

Encourage the students to **speculate** but not decide:
- Has something happened?
- Has the Bride run away?
- Was the Bride seen talking to someone?
- Has she had second thoughts?

Students **freeze or stop the drama.** The next part of the story is narrated by the teacher.

The Bride was never found and as the years passed, rumour and speculation surrounding the Bridegroom and his missing Bride continued to be a source of mystery and intrigue.

Several years later someone decided to clear out an unused room in the castle. Whilst moving furniture and pulling down old curtains and dusty tapestries, they found an old wooden chest pushed into a shadowy corner beneath several old curtains. Inside the chest was a skeleton.
The tattered remains of a white lace dress could be seen, and a circlet of dry flowers was still visible on the head.

Some versions of the legend refer to scratches on the inside of the chest and a gold ring on the finger of the skeleton.

Ask the students to think about the skeleton.

Some suggestions:
- Is the skeleton the missing Bride?
- If not who is it? Did the Bride persuade a friend (or order a servant) to swap clothes and hide in the chest?
- If so, why? As a joke or a distraction to enable her to run away, or some other reason. If she ran away, why and was she alone?
- If it is someone else in the chest why did no-one notice they were missing? Servants were considered unimportant so might not be searched for, perhaps people were too busy looking for the Bride or perhaps everyone assumed the Bride and the other missing person had run away together.
- What happened to the person in the chest?
- Were they alive when they went into the chest? Did they climb into the chest willingly? Did they fall asleep? Did they become trapped or were they deliberately locked in? If so, who locked them in and why?

In groups students prepare a **polished improvisation** to show what they think happened. Students can retain their original role or change to suit the roles required for their group drama. Students can now adopt the roles of the Bride, the Groom and people not yet mentioned in the story.

Share work from each group.

Extension

To develop the theme over more than one session explore the probability of who was in the chest and why they were there.

Hold a courtroom drama to determine who was responsible. As teacher you can take on the role of Judge or select a student.

Before heading to court decide who the suspects would be in this crime?

For example:
- The Bridegroom.
- The Bride.
- A friend.
- A servant.
- A former boyfriend...

Was this an accident or a deliberate act?
What was the motive?
- Jealousy
- Revenge
- Money
- To keep a secret...

Determine a list of suspects and assign roles to students. Remember to include witnesses.

You can either let the courtroom scenario unfold and follow where the story leads or use polished improvisations in small groups to show snapshots of the trial.

If students are unfamiliar with courtroom procedure use prompt cards.
Prompt cards must state clearly whether a character is guilty or innocent, the template I use is provided.

If using cards, the student on trial must keep the information regarding their guilt or innocence secret, of course the jury could still decide an innocent character is guilty or that the guilty person is innocent! I once held a trial for Macbeth, and he was found not guilty on all charges!

As a way of including the entire class, while eliminating a cast of thousands and a trial which would last the entire year, allocate one student to be the character voice but provide the 'voice' with a small support group. The group work together to decide where the character was, who they saw, what they heard, what they did etc. When they are questioned in court the supporters stand behind the character and can whisper suggestions to help answer questions.

In the same way the Defence and Prosecution can have a team to support them when planning their questions.

After each character has been questioned record brief versions of their answers and use these points at the end to determine a verdict.

It is a good idea to limit either the number of questions or time allowed to question and cross examine characters.

Differentiation

Support given by the teacher, especially while the teacher is in role and by the arrangement of groups.

Allocation of roles during the trial.

Use of prompt cards.

Background information regarding the time period can be provided.

Links to other curriculum areas /literacy tasks

Music – look at the music associated with 'The Mistletoe Bough.' Learn the song, create a modern version.

History – explore life for different types of people during the 1800s. Visit an old castle and explore the history of the building / architecture. Investigate the back story to the legend.

Art - look at the clothes worn during the time period and design the Bride's dress. Design the wedding invitations.

Design Technology – make 3D models of the castle.

Create a modern version of the legend.

Use artistic license to mix time periods and consider who / what type of people would be guests at the wedding. Produce a celebrity magazine such as *OK* or *Hello* with articles about the ceremony, guests and the disappearance of the young Bride.

Quick Ideas

Some teachers like to have a short warm-up before a drama lesson, personally I've never found the need to do this. However, warm-ups can be useful icebreakers if you find yourself running a Drama Club or if you are working with a new group of students who don't know each other.

Below are some quick and easy ideas.

Find Your Group

This activity is a good way to make students mix and interact with other students, it forces them to break away from only working with their friends.

Students stand in a circle. The teacher places a coloured sticky dot or star on the forehead of each student, taking care to ensure a good mix of colours. In silence, students must identify the colour they have been assigned and form a group with others of the same colour.

The activity can be varied by:

- A minimum and maximum number of students per group.
- The group must contain a specified number of people but must only have one member of each colour.
- There must be at least one girl / boy / someone with long hair / glasses...

This can be a way to divide the class into groups, a stand-alone task for students who have not met or worked together, or it can become part of a lesson about discrimination / popularity / bullying...

If you know the class and are happy that a student will cope with being left out choose one student to be the only one assigned a particular colour. This is a good springboard for a lesson or discussion about feelings and prejudice. It is a lesson I have used with Year Five and with GCSE students.

With older students I arrange the students facing out of the circle and I walk behind them, putting the sticker on their back to avoid them trying to see the colour I have selected from the sheet.

Wink Murder

This is an old one and was a common party game when I was younger. I have included it here because a surprising number of people have heard of, but never played this game.

Students sit or stand in a circle, and the teacher secretly selects a student to be the murderer. The murderer winks at other students who then 'die' as dramatically as possible. The winner is the last person 'alive.'

A variation is to send two students out of the room before the murderer is selected. These students are the detectives and must try to find the murderer as quickly as possible.

As in the previous activity, I ask the students to face outward while I walk around the inside of the circle. I select the murderer by tapping a student on the shoulder.

Choosing two (or multiple) murderers without telling anyone adds another layer of interest, as does making the identity of the detectives a secret. To do this I usually tap someone on the shoulder once to identify them as the murderer and twice to select a detective.

Alternatively, once the murderer(s) and detectives have been selected break up the circle and rather than sitting, students wander around the room trying to kill or avoid being killed.

As with the other ideas, this can be integrated into other lessons.

For example:
Using the game as a stimulus to discuss suspicion is a good way to introduce the theme of Witchcraft.

Using Levels

Using levels can add visual interest and can be used to symbolise or signify status and power. However, from a drama, rather than theatre perspective, levels give students an emotional link to the status of their character.

> **For example:**
> - When Lady Macbeth is persuading her husband to kill Duncan try the dialogue first with her standing on a chair looking down towards her husband, then again with the positions reversed.
> - For a lesson about bullying or coercion position a student at a lower level and have those students representing bullies higher.
> - If you are using The Crucible as a GCSE Drama text, sit the accused character on the lowest level and have the girls who are the accusers moving in a circle around the character on the ground. As they circle around the accused, students should shout their accusations. Discuss how this makes the person in the centre of the circle feel.
> - In a similar manner to the last point encourage the students to move randomly around the space adopting higher and lower positions as they call out accusations.

Character / Behaviour Prompts

Giving students a card, which directs them to behave in a certain manner can add a layer of intrigue to whole class dramas, it also encourages less confident students to take a more active role.

These prompts can be given to the entire class or only to selected students.

Using The 'What If?' Scenario

I love asking, *'What if?'* as a stimulus. With younger students, use familiar stories and fairytales, with older students anything from current affairs to exam texts can be used. This also provides an excellent creative writing task.

For example:
- What if the wolf only wanted to borrow a cup of sugar from the three pigs?
- What if there was a witness when Macbeth stabbed Duncan?

Courtroom Drama

A public meeting or trial can be used in many situations to bring a whole class drama to a climax or as a way of developing a what if scenario. I have mentioned this convention and pointed out ways to involve as many students as possible in the lesson using *The Mistletoe Bough*.

A courtroom drama is a useful way to explore characters and 'what if' scenarios from most stories or poems. Select the character to be put on trial, then decide who the witnesses would be and follow the format used with *The Mistletoe Bough*.

Sometimes an entire trial is not necessary, and characters can be **hot seated** briefly to gain an insight into their actions and possible motivations.

The **Magistrates** run a **Mock Trial** Competition in most areas for students aged between 12 and 14, the **Bar Association** run a **Mock Trial** Competition for older students from ages 15 to 18. They provide excellent resources and support to schools taking part.

Character / Behaviour Prompt Suggestion Cards

Sneeze whenever you are standing beside someone with a ponytail.	Never remain in a group with two or more other people.	Ask the person to your left if they would like a cup of tea? If they say yes, mime preparing one.	If you ask a question speak normally, if you answer a question you must sing.
Check your watch whenever someone coughs.	You are desperate to be best friends with anyone wearing glasses.	Identify one person in the room and follow them everywhere.	Pretend to be too hot.
Cough whenever someone sneezes.	You are terrified of anyone who coughs.	Whenever you move, pretend to be riding a horse.	Pretend to be too cold.
Cross the room and walk away from the group if anyone sneezes.	Always try to be in a group of three or more people.	Whenever you move, pretend to be walking a tightrope.	Ask as many questions as you can.
You are terrified of anyone with long hair.	You are desperate to be best friends with anyone who has long hair.	If you need to speak you must whisper.	Smile, sympathetically.

Courtroom Role Cards

You are innocent. You must answer all questions truthfully. **You will be referred to as The Defendant.**	**You are guilty.** You can answer truthfully or lie. **You will be referred to as The Defendant.**	**You are a witness.** You are not on trial. You must answer all questions truthfully.
You are the Judge. You must listen carefully to the questions asked by the Defence and Prosecution. You can make notes. You must ensure everyone behaves. You settle any arguments and help the Jury understand what is happening. You do not decide whether the accused is guilty or not guilty, but you do decide the punishment.	**You are a Magistrate.** There is no Jury in a Magistrates Court, you decide whether the person in court is 'guilty' or 'not guilty' after hearing evidence from the Prosecution and the Defence. The Head Magistrate has the deciding vote if the other two Magistrates do not agree.	**You are a Magistrate.** There is no Jury in a Magistrates Court, you decide whether the person in court is 'guilty' or 'not guilty' after hearing evidence from the Prosecution and the Defence. The Head Magistrate has the deciding vote if the other two Magistrates do not agree.
You are The Prosecution Barrister. You are trying to show how the Defendant has broken the law. It is your role to present enough convincing evidence against the Defendant to persuade the Jury to find the Defendant guilty.	**You are the Head Magistrate.** There is no Jury in a Magistrates Court, you decide whether the person in court is 'guilty' or 'not guilty' after hearing evidence from the Prosecution and the Defence. Sit between the other Magistrates. The Head Magistrate has the deciding vote if the other two Magistrates do not agree.	**You are the Court Clerk.** You sit at the front of the court and makes sure the Magistrates have all the information required during the trial. You also read out the charge to the Defendant. At the end of the trial, you give a of the case. **You can make notes to help.**

You are the Defence Barrister. You represent the person accused of committing the crime. You do not have to prove the Defendant's innocence. You point out to the Jury what is wrong with the Prosecution's arguments and why they are not convincing enough. A Defence Barrister's arguments are called the 'case for the defence' and will try to offer other explanations and show someone other than the accused could have committed the crime.	**You are a member of the Jury.** You decide if the defendant is guilty and must come to a decision after listening to all witnesses and arguments from the Defence Barrister and Prosecution Barrister. Every Jury nominates one member to be a foreman. Their court role is being the spokesperson that the Judge asks to deliver the Jury's decision to the court. There are twelve members of the Jury.	**You are a Court Reporter.** Court reporters work for either the local or national press, radio, TV and online reports. Court reporters are not allowed to take any photographs in the courtroom. You can make sketches and ask anyone for comment, apart from Magistrates.
You are the Usher. You make sure witnesses, and the public know where to sit. You carry written questions from the Jury to the Judge. You tell everyone in the courtroom to stand when the Judge or Magistrates enter or leave the court. You escort the Witnesses to and from the witness box. You take the oaths or affirmations from Witnesses and the Jury.	**The Oath / Affirmation to swear in Witnesses:** "I swear that the evidence I am about to give is the truth, the whole truth and nothing but the truth."	**The Oath / Affirmation to swear in Jury Members:** "I swear that I will faithfully try the defendant and give a true verdict according to the evidence."

Writing Frame Newspaper

The Daily News

Breaking News

Write your main headline here.

Pull quote.

Photograph / image.

Caption.

And Finally...

To conclude I have one more 'What if?'

What if it all goes wrong?

Occasionally things will not go to plan, but this is true of any lesson whatever the subject. If a science experiment does not work teachers will usually use the 'failure' as a learning opportunity and analyse, with the class, the reasons why the experiment did not work as expected; if things go wrong in drama, we can do the same.

The students might not respond to the stimulus, or the lack of engagement might be as a result of behaviour issues. In my experience, students usually prefer to co-operate and help keep the drama going, rather than spend the lesson writing or discussing what went wrong.

What should I do?
- Accept the lesson cannot be retrieved and discuss with the class the reasons.
- Complete self-analysis sheets.
- Re-direct the drama by inserting a flashback.
- Allow the drama to take a completely different direction to your original plan. This might require some quick thinking, but if the students are taking ownership of the drama and making suggestions, they've done most of the work for you.
- If a student tries to disrupt the flow of the lesson, use a spot of reverse psychology and follow their lead. Take a deep breath and put the disruptive student in a position of power.

I was struggling to engage a student when using the Mistletoe Bough idea, so I made him the key witness. On another occasion the disruptive student was allocated the role of the Judge in a courtroom drama. The Judge doesn't actually do a lot but looks important and I was able to stand close by.

Remember, Drama as a tool for learning does not need to last an entire lesson, it can be a quick five-minute part of the lesson.

About the Author

Catherine Rix was born in South Shields where she lived and worked until moving with her husband and daughter from Tyneside to the neighbouring county of Northumberland. After qualifying as a teacher with a B.Ed. (Hons.) Degree she worked as a teacher of English and Drama in a range of schools across the North East of England. In 2017 Catherine took a leap of faith and is now living the dream, working as a writer, deep in the heart of Northumberland.

Visit:
Catherinerix.wixsite.com/author
Instagram: catherinerix_author
Facebook: Catherine Rix – Author

Printed in Great Britain
by Amazon

41797684R00035